IN FOCUS

Time to re-charge those batteries!

Hello! I'm Lektron the robot and I'd like to welcome you to *In Focus.* I hope you're all switched on and tuned in, because this issue of *The Navigator* is all about keeping a close eye on the things around us and looking at what they tell us. Prepare for lift-off as we journey to the largest-ever model of the solar system. You'll also be blown away by the explosive article on fireworks. I'll even introduce you to some of my cyber chums, who can walk and talk like you. But only if you remember to switch them on!

Have a blast!

Text Type	Literacy Skills	Wider Curriculum Links
Persuasive	Information retrieval; deductive comprehension; making comparisons; expressing and justifying opinions	**History** Unit 11: What was it like for children living in Victorian Britain?
Recount (visual)	Inferential and deductive comprehension; expressing and justifying opinions	**History** Unit 11: What was it like for children living in Victorian Britain?
Report	Information retrieval	**Science** Unit 5E: Earth, Sun and Moon
Report/ Persuasive	Interpreting information; language analysis	**Art and Design** Unit 5A: Objects and meanings
Report	Understanding authorial intent; expressing and justifying opinions; information retrieval	**Design and Technology** Unit 5C: Moving toys
Report/ Persuasive	Information retrieval; comparing information; interpreting information	**Geography** Unit 18: Connecting ourselves to the world
Persuasive/ Report	Distinguishing between fact and opinion; information retrieval; comparing information; interpreting information	**Geography** Unit 18: Connecting ourselves to the world
Report	Information retrieval; interpreting information	**Geography** Unit 11: Water
Explanation	Interpreting information	**Art and Design** Unit 5B: Containers
Explanation	Summarising information; expressing and justifying opinions	**PSHE:** Developing a healthy, safer lifestyle; preparing to play an active role as citizens
Fun spread		
		ICT: Year 5 Schemes of work

The latest things...

Here are some adverts from a Victorian ladies' magazine. Would any of these 'latest things' tempt you to part with your pocket money?!

SOUTHALL'S PATENT WINDOW CLEANER

Is it possible that any lady will let her servant run the risk of being killed, when the small sum of 7s 6d will make the risk unnecessary?

MARY: Lawks Bridget! How can you stand out there like that? Why don't you ask your mistress to buy a nice machine like this? It does inside and out in a wink, no fear of breaking the glass, and you don't need to go out at all.

BRIDGET: Sure and the mistress is too careful of her money. Anyhow, if I'm killed my man Micky'll make them pay! Sure and it's bad news about the window. Look it's smashed and I only touched it!

SOUTHALL BROS., Sole Makers, Headingly, Leeds

MADAME DOWDING

8 & 10, CHARING CROSS ROAD (Opposite the National Gallery, Trafalgar Square)
Tailor, Corsetiere and Court Dressmaker

No.3 - THE KITCHENER

Sure to be a great favourite with military men. Helps to give the correct carriage in all circumstances.
Suitable for hunting. Elasticated panels for ease of movement.
Priced from 50 shillings.

No. 8 - THE IMPROVED REJANE CORSET
For obesity

Several West End doctors declare this to be the most perfect anatomical corset yet invented for ladies inclined to be overweight.
Priced from 38 shillings.

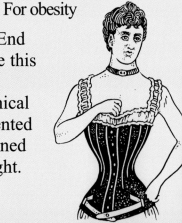

4

The Victorians liked to stress that they were living in an age of invention. People loved to own 'the latest things'. The Victorian period was also the time when more and more people, especially women, learned to read and write. For the first time, newspapers and magazines were printed in large quantities and with illustrations. It was not surprising, then, that businesses decided to use magazines and newspapers to advertise their inventions.

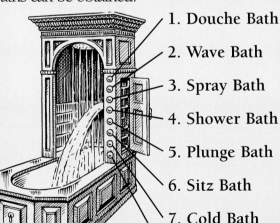

The Cadbury brothers

The Cadbury family were Quakers, a religious group who believed in fighting poverty and injustice. John Cadbury was a Birmingham grocer who, in 1831, switched to making drinking chocolate and cocoa. In 1847 his sons, George and Richard, moved the business to a bigger factory. But by the late 1870s, this factory had become too small and the brothers decided to build a new one …

1878

> Richard, why not build our new factory in the countryside?

> An excellent idea, George! The countryside will be better for our workers' health than the filthy air of Birmingham!

The Cadbury brothers, unlike many factory owners, treated their workers well. They were paid reasonable wages, only worked a half day on Saturdays, and had Sundays and bank holidays off.

1880

The factory was built near the Worcester Canal, which ran all the way to the Bristol Docks. It was also near a road and a railway line. When the factory opened, it had 230 workers. Houses for 24 of the workers were built near the factory straight away.

> Our factory is making good money. Our workers seem very happy.

> Yes, Richard. Let's move more workers out here, to live near the factory.

In 1895, the Cadbury brothers bought 140 acres of land, and began to build a village. In the first year, 143 houses were built. The houses were sold at the price they cost to build – around £150 each.

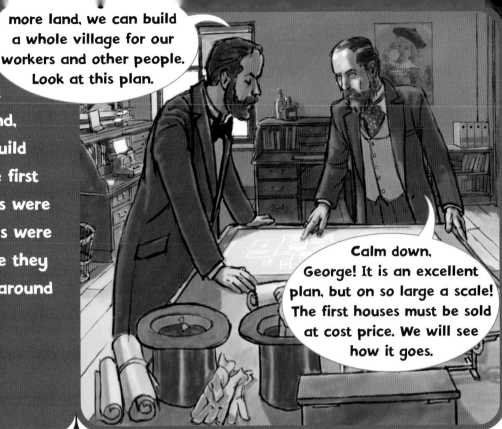

"more land, we can build a whole village for our workers and other people. Look at this plan."

"Calm down, George! It is an excellent plan, but on so large a scale! The first houses must be sold at cost price. We will see how it goes."

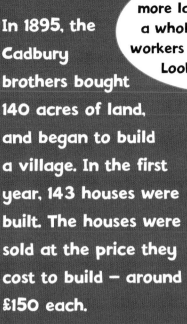

"How well Bournville Village has worked! There are all kinds of houses to rent and buy, and the school and hospital are working well."

"Yes. I worry it has been too successful, Richard. People are buying houses here to sell at a profit. Something must be done!"

1900

By 1900, Bournville Village covered 330 acres. There were over 300 houses. People were buying homes in the village to sell at a profit. So the Cadbury brothers set up the Bournville Village Trust. The Trust ran the village the way the Cadbury brothers wanted it run – to help people. It still does today.

How big is the solar system? You can get a good idea by visiting Otford, a village in Kent, which has the largest-ever scale model of the solar system. The model is built to a scale of 2.5 cm to 128 000 km. As a visit to the village shows, that makes the solar system a mind-boggling size.

The model stretches over a distance of nearly a kilometre. The Sun is at the centre of the model, and Pluto, the most distant planet from the Sun, is in the middle of field on the outskirts of the village.

The model was the idea of David Thomas, a retired teacher, and Barry Keenan, an amateur astronomer. They wanted to find a unique way to mark the millennium. Their idea was to calculate the sizes and positions of the planets at midnight on 1 January 2001. When they had done this, they positioned markers round the village. The four inner planets – Mercury, Mars, Earth and Venus, the planets which are nearest to the Sun – are all on the village recreation ground. Jupiter, the largest planet in the solar system is 186 metres away from the Sun, while Saturn is more than 330 metres away, outside the doctor's surgery.

David Thomas and Barry Keenan

Now David Thomas and Barry Keenan plan to extend their model to include the nearest star to the solar system. Proxima Centauri, is about 40 million million kilometres away from the Earth. On the same scale as the Otford model, that is about 8000 km. This means that the model of this star will be in Lo Angeles, in California, USA.

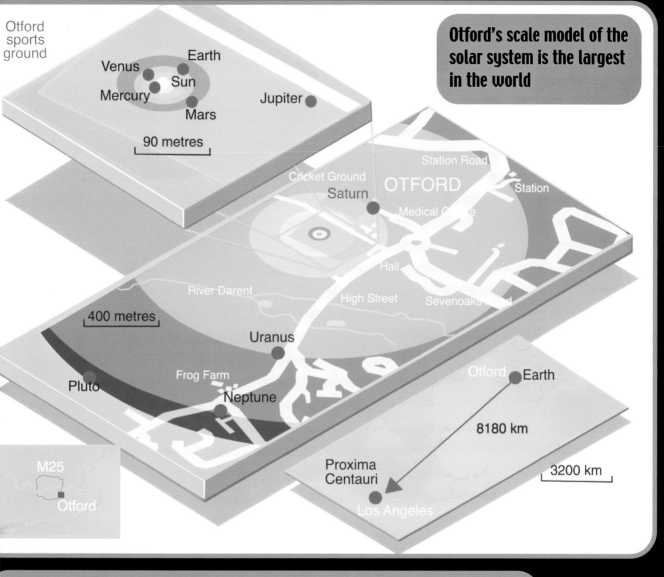

Otford sports ground

Venus
Earth
Mercury
Sun
Mars
Jupiter

90 metres

Otford's scale model of the solar system is the largest in the world

Station Road
Cricket Ground
OTFORD
Saturn
Station
Medical Centre

Hall
River Darent
High Street
Sevenoaks Road

400 metres

Uranus
Frog Farm
Otford
Earth
Pluto
Neptune

8180 km

M25
Otford

Proxima Centauri
Los Angeles

3200 km

The Solar System – showing distance from the sun

Sun

Mercury
58 million km

Venus
108 million km

Earth
150 million km

Mars
228 million km

Jupiter
778 million km

Saturn
1427 million km

Uranus
2870 million km

Neptune
4497 million km

Pluto
5900 million km

9

Draw and Paint

~ A catalogue for artists ~

Flexible friend

Degas went to the ballet, Lautrec visited theatres and bars, Picasso used live models. You can manipulate this jointed figure to simulate human mobile, acrobatic or static poses. The metal mount and wooden base ensure stability.

Flexible figure, wood, 30cm
Order No: X0022   £12.00

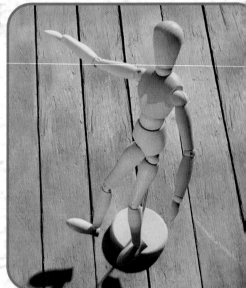

Rainbow colours

Monet used oil paints. You can reproduce a similar spectrum of colours with these oil pastels. Smooth to apply, they come in a range of colours not usually associated with 'pastels'.

Boxed set, 12, 24, 48
Order No: C0014/15/16

[for prices see reverse of order form]

Synthetic, but naturally the best

The Dutch masters relied on costly, natural ingredients to mix their own colours. These easy-to-apply acrylic paints are available in over 50 shades. Undiluted, they give the same rich, deep areas of colour. Mixed with water, they can effectively reproduce watercolour or wash. **Acrylic paints, available in 38ml, 60ml, 118ml tubes.   Order No: C0008**

[for prices of 38ml, 60ml & 118ml tubes see reverse of order form]

The real thing

For centuries, artists from Van Eyck to Van Gogh have used brushes made from hog's hair. Quality does not come cheaply, but purchase the whole set and the fifth brush comes absolutely free. **Set of 5 hog's hair brushes** (varying widths) **Order No: X0004   £39.95**

Instant art

From 17th century Holland to 20th century New York, artists have incorporated lettering into their works of art. Easy to transfer onto most surfaces, this lettering comes in a selection of typefaces and sizes. Each set contains upper and lower case letters and numbers, with approximately ten duplicates.

Transfer lettering Order No: X0035 [for prices see reverse of order form]

HI-TECH

Our Navigator team has been hard at work testing these cool cyber pets. Which would you give your star rating to?

WALKING RAPTOR

DESCRIPTION This scary reptile starts life quite vicious, so watch out for his attacks. Raptor will respond to your commands, petting and having his tail pulled.

BEST FEATURE Scarily real!

WORST FEATURE He might bite the postman!

PRICE £99.99

THE NAVIGATOR RATING

★ ★ ★ ★ ★

I-CYBIE

DESCRIPTION The leader of the pack, i-Cybie can do everything the others can but better! He even detects objects in his way and changes direction. If he falls over, he can get up again by himself!

BEST FEATURE If he was furry you'd never know the difference between him and a real-life rover!

WORST FEATURE His price tag.

PRICE £179.99

THE NAVIGATOR RATING

★ ★ ★ ★ ★

PETS!

Check out our rating system guide:

★ ★ ★ ★ ★ Top dog!
★ ★ ★ ★ ☆ Cyber-cool!
★ ★ ★ ☆ ☆ Worth a walk
★ ★ ☆ ☆ ☆ Steer clear
★ ☆ ☆ ☆ ☆ In the dog house!

SHELBY

DESCRIPTION
This clever urchin can speak Shelbish, Furbish and English. It can also play games, but be gentle, or Shelby will clam up!
BEST FEATURE Can communicate with other Shelbys and Furbies.
WORST FEATURE None!
PRICE £24.99
THE NAVIGATOR RATING
★ ☆ ★ ☆ ☆

TEKSTA

DESCRIPTION This playful pooch can wag his tail, bark, cry and growl.
BEST FEATURE His nose sensor – press it and he sniffs!
WORST FEATURE He can be programmed to wake you up in the mornings.
PRICE £39.99
THE NAVIGATOR RATING
★ ★ ★ ★ ☆

SONY AIBO

DESCRIPTION Aibo has got tiny cameras in his eyes that record his movements so you can play back his photograhic diary through them! He'll dance and play games too!
BEST FEATURE He can recognise up to 50 words.
WORST FEATURE You can't buy one! These pooches were only sold in America.
PRICE £1500 (real dogs are a lot cheaper!)
THE NAVIGATOR RATING
★ ☆ ☆ ☆ ☆

DOG.E

DESCRIPTION With a remote control, you can steer Dog.e all over the place. He moves his ears, wags his tail and even carries things in his mouth!
BEST FEATURE The sounds he makes while eating and drinking.
WORST FEATURE Bit pricey.
PRICE £59.99
THE NAVIGATOR RATING
★ ★ ☆ ☆ ☆

BLUE PINE ACTIVITY CENTRE

An activity holiday is the experience of a lifetime.
If you've never been on one, now's your chance to try!
Read the brochures for two activity centres offering this kind of holiday.
Which one would you most like to visit?

School trips to the Blue Pine Activity Centre are educational **and** fun. They are an excellent way for children and teachers to get to know each other better. That's why many schools make repeat bookings year after year after year.

Location A beautiful 20-acre park overlooking a lake near Ben Gavor, one of Scotland's highest mountains. Spectacular mountain scenery with steep gorges, tumbling rivers and lakes.

Activities Exciting seasonal and year-round activities led by fully-trained instructors at all levels from beginner to advanced, including:
• Horse riding • Skiing • Rock climbing
• Mountain craft (e.g. navigation, ice axe work, avalanche awareness)
• Canoeing with overnight camping

Visitors We take school groups only for weekend visits or Monday-to-Friday. All travel to be arranged by visiting schools.

Accommodation A handsome shooting lodge built in the 1930s, with all modern facilities. Sleeps up to 54 guests in basic but comfortable rooms. All rooms have carpet, wash-hand basin and bunk beds, with all bedding supplied.

Food Three healthy, home-cooked meals a day including breakfast, picnic lunch and evening meal.

Facilities Games room with table tennis • Sports hall: football, volleyball, badminton • Games field • Abseil facility • Communal dining room • Drying room

Camp rules No radios or CD players • No television • No smoking • No alcohol • Visitors are asked to help lay tables and wash up • Lights out at 11 pm

CLUB CICADA

Activities

f you like water, you'll love our activities. They nclude:
- Swimming • Snorkelling • Windsurfing
- Water-skiing • Sailing • Beach volleyball

All our groups are led by trained instructors. All activities are optional. You are free to elax on the beach if you prefer!

Our summer paradise offers visitors freedom, fun, excitement and the chance to make new friends!

Location
Our camp is in the south of France, beside a sandy beach and the warm blue water of the Mediterranean Sea. The small nearby town of Sanary-les-Pins is just a 10-minute walk away.

Visitors
We welcome visitors aged 8–13 who are able to swim 50 metres. Friends/siblings can be accommodated together. Holidays last for 8 days including travel, with 6 nights at the camp. May–September only.

Accommodation
Comfortable 4 berth-tents with camp beds. Visitors need to bring their own sleeping bag and pillow.

Food
Three meals a day: cooked breakfast, packed lunch, cooked dinner, late drinks. Vegetarian alternatives available.

Facilities
Hot showers and toilet facilities.
Bar and disco area with discos every night!
Covered dining tent.

Travel
By luxury coach (20 hours) with seat belts, WC and video, plus ferry crossing.

With so much to do at activity centres, it can be hard to know what to try. How fit do you need to be for each activity? What equipment do you need? What can you hope to achieve? The following fact sheets answer these and other questions. So take your time to read them – and then choose your activity!

WIND-SURFING

Can you swim 50 metres?
Do you have stamina and determination?
Do you enjoy falling into the water?

Then you'll love wind-surfing!

We provide:
• top-quality wind-surfing gear: wet suit, buoyancy aid, windsurfer board and rig
• qualified instructors
• the safe, calm waters of the lake

You will need:
• swimming costume
• pair of plimsolls
• towel
• fingerless gloves (optional)

You will learn how to:
• rig a windsurfer
• launch it on the water
• get on board
• sail with the wind
• change direction
• return to shore
• respect other water users

By the end of the week:
You will be windsurfing out on the lake and coming back safely to shore.

HORSE RIDING

Do you enjoy being out in the open air, exploring beautiful countryside? Do you like horses and ponies? Are you reasonably fit and healthy?

Then horse riding may be for you!

We provide:
- all equipment: hard hat, boots, tack
- a good selection of horses for a variety of riders
- top-quality instruction

You will learn how to:
- handle horses safely and confidently
- groom your own horse
- care for tack
- tack up
- mount a horse
- be balanced in the saddle
- walk, trot and canter

By the end of the week:
You will feel confident around horses, and will be trekking along local bridle paths and riding on nearby hills.

SKIING

Are you fairly confident? Are you reasonably fit and healthy? Do you enjoy fresh air and the beauty of the mountains?

Then why not give skiing a try?

We provide:
- top-quality equipment: skis, poles, boots
- ski suit
- lift pass
- qualified instruction

You will need:
- sunglasses
- sun protection
- gloves
- warm hat and socks

You will learn how to:
- put on and carry your skis
- use a chair lift
- move around on skis
- fall in a controlled way
- get up after a fall
- make a turn and stop safely
- ski down a slope
- respect other skiers

By the end of the week:
You will have a good grasp of the basics and enjoy skiing down a mountain slope.

WET, WET WORLD!

Did you know that about two-thirds of your body is made of water? Or that the water you drink from the tap is at least 3000 million years old – it's been recycled in clouds and rainfall since it first appeared on the Earth. Read on to discover more fascinating facts about the world of water!

WHAT A LOT OF SALT

Water covers more than two-thirds of our planet, and most of this water can be found in the seas. If you could fit all the water in the world into a four-litre container, the fresh water would amount to just over a tablespoon. The water that is frozen into ice would fill half a cup. All the rest of it would be salty seawater.

sea water (97.5%)

4 litres
3 litres
2 litres
1 litre

fresh water (0.5%)

ice (2%)

Pacific Ocean

THE WORLD'S SEAS

The world's largest ocean is the Pacific Ocean. It covers nearly a third of the Earth's surface.

Eiffel Tower

325 metre

Marianas Trench

The deepest part of the deepest ocean is the Marianas Trench in the Pacific Ocean. It is 11 km deep. If you stacked 35 Eiffel Towers on top of each other on the seabed, they would just reach the surface.

WATER ON THE MOVE

The world's longest river is the River Nile. It is 6670 km long, and flows from Lake Victoria in Africa to the Mediterranean Sea. If it was straight, it would stretch from London to Chicago!

The route of the Nile

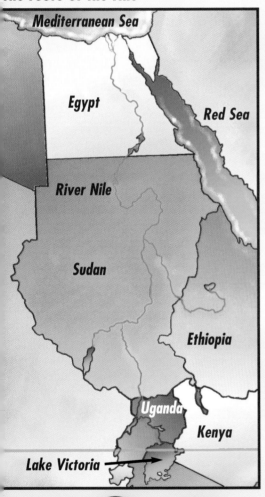

Mediterranean Sea

Egypt

Red Sea

River Nile

Sudan

Ethiopia

Uganda

Kenya

Lake Victoria

The world's shortest river is the D River in the USA. It's just 37 m long – that's the same length as ten canoes.

The world's highest waterfall is Angel Falls in Venezuela in South America. It drops 979 m – that's more than twice the height of the Empire State Building!

Angel Falls

The rainiest place in the world is Mount Wai-'ale-'ale in Hawaii. It rains on 350 days of the year.

FROM CLOUD TO TAP

Rain falls from a cloud, and runs into rivers or soaks into the ground. It is then pumped up into pipes.

▼

The water is poured into huge tanks. The dirt in the water sinks to the bottom and is removed.

▼

The water is then strained through layers of sand and stones. It is treated with bleach to kill off germs.

▼

The clean water is piped to reservoirs and water towers. From there, it is pumped into large pipes called mains.

▼

The water mains are joined to small pipes in your house. When you turn on the tap, the water pours out!

Pear in a bottle

Pear brandy is sometimes sold with a whole pear inside the bottle. How do they get the pear inside?

1 Pear trees flower in the spring. When the petals have fallen, the pears begin to grow. Glass bottles are placed over the pears, and tied to the branches with string.

Stripes in toothpaste

Some kinds of toothpaste have different coloured stripes. How do they get inside the tube without mixing together?

1 At the factory, the toothpaste is made in two colours, each in a separate mixer.

Ship in a bottle

Have you ever seen miniature ships inside small glass bottles? How do the tall masts and billowing sails squeeze through the bottle's narrow neck?

1 The ships are made by expert model makers. First, the diameter of the bottle and its neck are measured.

2 Then coloured putty is pushed inside the bottle, using special long-handled

2 During the summer, the pears continue to grow normally inside the bottles.

3 Just before the pears ripen, the stalks that hold them onto

the branches are cut. The pears remain inside the bottles.

4 The pears and the bottles are then cleaned by hand, using specially designed tools.

5 Finally, the bottles are filled with pear brandy and sealed tightly with a cork.

2 The two different coloured pastes are sent along separate pipes to the tube-filling machine. This has special nozzles designed to keep the two colours separate.

3 The tubes are filled and sealed at the bottom. The pastes are just stiff enough to remain separate, so the two colours don't mix together.

4 When the toothpaste is squeezed out of the tube, the stripes are still perfect!

ools. It is painted to look like the sea.

3 A tiny scale model of a ship is made. The masts are fixed to the ship's deck using tiny hinges, which allow them to fold flat against the deck. Threads are ied round the masts.

4 The ship is slid through the neck of the bottle and pressed onto the putty, making sure that the ends of the threads are still outside the bottle. The threads are then pulled to raise the masts and sails.

5 The threads are stuck into the putty, then trimmed with long, narrow scissors. Finally, the bottle is sealed with a cork.

HOW FIREWORKS WORK

Have you ever wondered how fireworks explode and make such lovely patterns?
All fireworks work in roughly the same way and contain the same basic ingredient which causes explosions. The ingredient is called gunpowder. It's the shape of the container that makes the different patterns.

Fireworks come in many different shapes and sizes.

The Chinese first started using gunpowder to make noisy fireworks to scare away evil spirits.

What is gunpowder?

Gunpowder is an explosive that blows up when it comes into contact with fire or high temperatures. The gunpowder is packed tightly into sealed containers, so when it explodes, it does so with tremendous force. The force is strong enough to blow the container apart or shoot it high into the sky.

Making different patterns

The fireworks that we see at public shows are known as 'display shells', and though they look spectacular, they are actually simple devices. Each is a simple tube or ball of cardboard filled with chemical pellets that burn when they are lit. These pellets, which are called 'stars', create the special effects in fireworks

Italian shells

These rockets are one of the most common types of display fireworks. The shell is made up of several parts.

stars ignite to produce a shower of light and colour

bursting charge — breaks shell open

second fuse —

stars —

launch tube —

first fuse —

gunpowder sends shell into sky

This is how a rocket works:

★ The first fuse runs inside the launch tube.

★ The gunpowder is ignited.

★ The powder explodes, launching the top half of the rocket into the sky and igniting the second fuse.

★ The second fuse sets off a chemical mixture called the 'bursting charge', which is packed around the stars.

★ The stars ignite, burst out of the shell and explode into the sky.

SAFETY NOTE

Remember, fireworks are dangerous. Always follow the Firework Code.

That's Magic

Now you see it, now you don't. It's magic! But how is it done? Magicians know better than to give away all their secrets, but here are few tricks of the trade.

★ Mind Reading

Baffle your audience with your mind-reading skills:
- First, ask a volunteer to point to an object when you have gone out of the room.
- Then leave the room and return a little while later.
- Now ask a second person to point to different objects until you identify the object the first volunteer pointed to.
- Look as if you are concentrating hard and then say 'Stop' when the person points to the correct object.

How did you do it?

It's easy – the second person is your accomplice! He or she gives you an agreed signal (such as crossing their legs) just before pointing to the correct object!

★ Rope Trick

Here's a really simple but effective trick. You are going to tie a knot in a piece of string without letting go of the ends. Sounds impossible?

You need a piece of rope or string about 1 metre long. Ask one or two members of your audience to try tying a knot in it without letting go of the ends.

You can be sure that they won't be able to do it. That's when you step in and show them how! Place the string on the table in front of you.

Fold your arms across your chest and pick up an end of the string in each hand. Unfold your arms and you will have tied a knot in the string. It's simple!

Here's a simple card trick. All you need is a pack of cards.

Before you start the trick, arrange the cards so that all the black cards are together at one end of the pack and all the red cards are together at the other end.

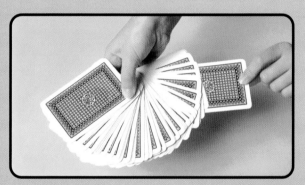

Ask someone to pick a card and remember what it is. Then ask him or her to put the card back into the pack without letting you see it.

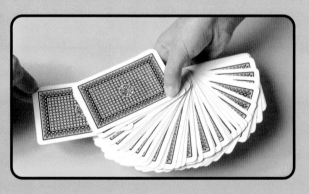

Offer the pack so that the card is put back in the other half of the pack. So, if the person took a card from the red end, make sure it is put back among the black cards.

Cut the pack a few times to make it look as though you are mixing the cards up. Then simply fan out the cards, making sure only you can see the faces, and dramatically pick out the chosen card!

Byte-Sized ICT

The latest things...

More inventions

Be a modern-day inventor! Just like the Victorians, people today still love to own 'the latest things'. Can you think of a fantastic new invention, designed to make life easier and to do the jobs we hate? How about an automatic bed-maker or a room-tidying robot?

Or why not come up with a fantastic health or beauty treatment to help people look or feel better? The Victorians loved these too! Just look back at the adverts for the bath on page 5.

When you have thought of an invention, use publishing software or a word-processor on your computer to design an eye-catching advert for your product. How will you persuade people to buy it? Will it make them feel happier, or save them time, or both? You could look at a selection of magazine and newspaper adverts to see what sort of phrases they use. Remember to use different font sizes to make important words and phrases stand out when people look at your advert.

The Cadbury brothers

ICT: Unit 5b Using complex searches

Chocolate recipes

Has the article about the Cadbury brothers got your mouth watering? Try searching the web for a recipe or two that use chocolate.

Remember, if you are using a search engine always include a couple of keywords to focus your search. You could try chocolate and recipes, for example. Don't forget to use 'and' to keep your search narrow.

Don't forget that there are lots of websites devoted to recipes that will appeal to young cooks. Once you have found the perfect recipe, all you need do is print it off and persuade someone at home to let you into the kitchen!

The Day the Earth Stood Still

ICT: Unit 5a Graphical modelling

Solar system challenge

An object-based drawing program allows you to move and change the things you have drawn. Try drawing a diagram of the solar system, keeping the planets approximately the right sizes in relation to each other and also the right distance apart. You can use the 'fill' tool to get them the right colour. This is often shown by a bucket icon on your screen. Don't forget to label the planets too!

You could even attempt to complete the diagram without looking back at the one in the book. When you have finished, save your work, then look back at the book and check it. Did you get the order and sizes of the planets right? Amend your work to make sure it is correct and print out both versions to compare.

This is the bucket icon.

Draw and Paint –
A catalogue for artists

Text testing

When you use a word-processor, do you always seem to use the same font? One that you know you like, or looks right? Or perhaps you are one of those people who uses the strangest looking font you can find! Here is the chance to change all that.

Spend some time exploring the different fonts available on your computer. When you have had a good look, choose five different ones. Produce a poster showing people what each font is like, and give a few suggestions for the kind of writing it might be best suited for.

For example, you could try finding a font suitable for a young children's book. For that, you would need to make sure it had clear and simple letters for them to read, without too many decorative loops or slanting letters. On the other hand, a font suitable for typing up some homework about a history topic could be fancier and more old-fashioned.

Wet wet world!

Water facts challenge

Find out three more interesting facts about water using an encyclopaedia CD-ROM. If you have a geography encyclopaedia on CD-ROM, or even an atlas, you could try finding out about seas, rivers or lakes. Or how about rainfall in different places?

If you have a science encyclopaedia, try searching for facts about the water cycle or the different states of water.

A general encyclopaedia might include all of these, although perhaps in less detail. Compare your results with a friend and discuss which sources were most useful.

How fireworks work

Keep safe

Design a firework safety poster using a word-processor or publishing software on your computer. You will need to find out a bit more about the firework code first, so try looking on the Internet.

Make sure your poster is bold and clear, and remember to think about who you want to read it. If it is for young children, think about how you can present the information in a way they will understand.

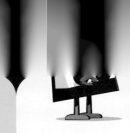

abseil	to lower yourself down a mountain or cliff, using a double rope
amateur	someone who does something interesting for fun, not for money
brandy	an alcoholic drink made from wine or fruit juice
corset	underwear that supports your waist, abdomen or upper legs
defects	faults or flaws
devices	mechanical tools
diameter	the distance across a circle or tube
dramatically	in a manner that is lively, forceful, exciting
duplicates	exact copies
factory	a building where something is made or put together
fuse	the wick used to ignite explosives
grocer	someone who sells food such as sugar or flour, and household goods such as soap
infections	diseases
manipulated	skilfully moved by hand
miniature	a much smaller version of something

mobile	able to move or be moved easily
nozzle	a spout at the end of a pipe or hose
obesity	extreme fatness
optional	you can choose
pellets	small round balls of something
putty	a soft paste, made from a mixture of oil and chalk, that goes hard when it is dry
shilling	a silver coin, worth about 10p, used in the United Kingdom before the introduction of decimal currency
solar system	the sun, and the planets, comets and asteroids that travel or orbit around it
spectrum	the seven colours into which white light is divided
stamina	the strength and power to keep going, especially when you are tired
static	not active, moving or changing
synthetic	artificially made
tack	the equipment used in horse riding, including the saddle and bridle
tandem	a bicycle for two riders